AF270347

Barbie

by Grace Hansen

Abdo Kids Jumbo is an Imprint of Abdo Kids
abdobooks.com

abdobooks.com

Published by Abdo Kids, a division of ABDO, P.O. Box 398166, Minneapolis, Minnesota 55439.
Copyright © 2023 by Abdo Consulting Group, Inc. International copyrights reserved in all countries.
No part of this book may be reproduced in any form without written permission from the publisher.
Abdo Kids Jumbo™ is a trademark and logo of Abdo Kids.

Printed in China.

102022

012023

THIS BOOK CONTAINS
RECYCLED MATERIALS

Photo Credits: AP Images, Getty Images, Shutterstock PREMIER

Production Contributors: Teddy Borth, Jennie Forsberg, Grace Hansen
Design Contributors: Candice Keimig, Pakou Moua

Library of Congress Control Number: 2022937185
Publisher's Cataloging-in-Publication Data

Names: Hansen, Grace, author.

Title: Barbie / by Grace Hansen

Description: Minneapolis, Minnesota : Abdo Kids, 2023 | Series: Toy mania! | Includes online resources and
    index.

Identifiers: ISBN 9781098264260 (lib. bdg.) | ISBN 9781098264826 (ebook) | ISBN 9781098265106
    (Read-to-Me ebook)

Subjects: LCSH: Barbie dolls--Juvenile literature. | Dolls--Juvenile literature. | Toys--Juvenile literature. |
    Mattel, Inc.--Juvenile literature.

Classification: DDC 688.722--dc23

Table of Contents

Barbie

Barbie stepped into the world in black high-heel sandals on March 9, 1959. She also wore a striped swimsuit and cat eye sunglasses. Barbie was very **fashionable** for the time. But she would go on to be so much more.

4

Barbie Is Born

Ruth Handler, her husband Elliot, and Harold Matson started Mattel Creations in 1945. They sold many popular toys. But Barbie would be one of their biggest hits.

MUSIC BOX
HURDY GURDY
Mattel Music
Super
MOVIE SHOW
COWBOY JOE'S
CHUCK WAGON
Farmer
Dell
PLAYS REAL MUSIC
FARMER IN THE DELL
THE MULBERRY BUSH
CART Jr.
DUCKS
PULL TOY

Ruth often saw her daughter, Barbara, and her friends play with dolls. They used their **imaginations**. But they soon tired of their dolls that looked too young. Ruth thought a grown-up doll might be more fun!

9

Mattel introduced Barbara
Millicent Roberts, Barbie for
short, in 1959. Girls were excited
about the **glamorous** doll. The
company sold 350,000 Barbie
dolls in the first year!

The first Barbie was meant to look like a 1950s movie star. But Ruth knew that girls would want Barbie to change just as the world did. First Lady Jackie Kennedy was a fashion icon in the early 1960s. Barbie's new wardrobe matched that.

GOOD GIRLS
BABY SI
Jackie Kennedy

Barbie would keep representing the most popular fashions through the decades. But Ruth wanted Barbie to be an important role model for girls too. So, Barbie took on many jobs.

bloom

Barbie's Dream World

Barbie has been a teacher, veterinarian, and surgeon. She was a flight attendant and airline pilot. Barbie went from businesswoman to rock star. She's mastered many sports and was even an Olympian!

YOU CAN BE
ANYTHING
Barbie
17

Mattel also creates Barbies that look like well-known people. The Inspiring Women Series **debuted** in 2018.

Barbie SIGNATURE
Sally Ride
ASTRONAUT
©2019 Mattel.
INSPIRING WOMEN™ SERIES
Barbie SIGNATURE
Rosa Parks
CIVIL RIGHTS ACTIVIST
Mattel.
INSPIRING WOMEN™ SERIES
Barbie SIGNATURE
Frida Kahlo
ARTIST
6+
INSPIRING WOMEN SERIES
SALLY RIDE   64,99 €
ROSA PARKS   64,99 €
FRIDA KAHLO   64,99 €
19

Since 1959, more than 1 billion Barbies have sold worldwide. Each day, kids everywhere are **inspired** by Barbie. There's no telling what she will do next!

More Facts

- According to the official Barbie website, Barbie is from the **fictional** town of Willows, Wisconsin.

- For the first 12 years of Barbie, the doll never smiled. In 1971, Malibu Barbie was introduced. She had a much happier look on her face!

- Barbie has had more than 40 pets! She has cared for 21 dogs, six cats, a parrot, and lots of farm animals.

Glossary

debuted – (of a product) launched or appeared in public for the first time.

fashionable – influenced by and dressing according to what is currently in style.

fictional – not existing in real life.

glamorous – full of fascination, allure, or excitement.

icon – a person who people recognize as a symbol of something. The person is often admired and respected.

imagination – the act or power of the mind to form a thought, picture, or image of something.

inspire – to influence or guide.

wardrobe – a collection of clothes or costumes.

Index

Visit **abdokids.com** to access crafts, games, videos, and more!